INVESTIGATING

CYBERCRIME

CRIME SCENE INVESTIGATORS

INVESTIGATING CYBERCRIME

Angie Timmons and Sara L. Latta

Enslow Publishing
101 W. 23rd Street
Suite 240
New York, NY 10011
USA
enslow.com

Published in 2018 by Enslow Publishing, LLC.
101 W. 23rd Street, Suite 240, New York, NY 10011

Library of Congress Cataloging-in-Publication Data

Names: Timmons, Angie, author. | Latta, Sara L., author.
Title: Investigating cybercrime / Angie Timmons and Sara L. Latta.
Description: New York, NY : Enslow Publishing, [2018] | Series: Crime scene investigators | Audience: Grades 5-8. | Includes bibliographical references and index.
Identifiers: LCCN 2017013607 | ISBN 9780766091832 (library bound) | ISBN 9780766095434 (paperback)
Subjects: LCSH: Computer crimes—Juvenile literature. | Criminal investigation—Juvenile literature. | Computer crimes—Prevention—Juvenile literature.
Classification: LCC HV6773 .T56 2018 | DDC 363.25/968—dc23
LC record available at https://lccn.loc.gov/2017013607

Printed in China

To Our Readers: We have done our best to make sure all website addresses in this book were active and appropriate when we went to press. However, the author and the publisher have no control over and assume no liability for the material available on those websites or on any websites they may link to. Any comments or suggestions can be sent by email to customerservice@enslow.com.

Portions of this book appeared in the book *Cybercrime: Data Trails Do Tell Tales.*

Photo Credits: Cover, pp. 3, 5, 6 (hooded figure, code) Benoit Daoust/Shutterstock.com; cover, p. 3 (taped laptop) Cheryl-Annette Parker/Shutterstock.com; cover and interior pages (magnifying glass) azure1/Shutterstock.com; pp. 8-9, 25, 73 © AP Images; p. 12 Ken Wolter/Shutterstock.com; p. 16 Nicholas Kamm/AFP/Getty Images; pp. 20-21 Oleh Slepchenko/Shutterstock.com; p. 23 Bettmann/Getty Images; p. 30 Owen Franken/Corbis Historical/Getty Images; pp. 34-35 Loftflow/Shutterstock.com; p. 36 JMiks/Shutterstock.com; p. 38 Bloomberg/Getty Images; p. 42 Boston Globe/Getty Images; p. 45 IIPA/Ebrahim Norouzi/AP Images; p. 50 Galerie Bilderwelt/Hulton Archvie/Getty Images; p. 51 bepsy/Shutterstock.com; p. 54 Richard Goerg/Photographer's Choice RF/Getty Images; pp. 56-57 Per-Anders Pettersson/Corbis Documentary/Getty Images; p. 59 Jerry Cleveland/The Denver Post/Getty Images; p. 62 Damien Meyer/AFP/Getty Images; p. 64 AF archive/Alamy Stock Photo; p. 66 GilC/Shutterstock.com; p. 69 Phil Walter/Getty Images; p. 76 Frederick M. Brown/Getty Images; pp. 77, 80-81 Monkey Business Images/Shutterstock.com; interior pages (keyboard) focuslight/Shutterstock.com; interior pages (handcuffs) Veronica Louro/Shutterstock.com.

CONTENTS

7 INTRODUCTION Computer Forensics: A Digital Crime Scene Investigator

11 CHAPTER 1 Cybercriminals Take the Bank for the Holidays

22 CHAPTER 2 The Early Days of Cybercrime

32 CHAPTER 3 The Internet of Things

43 CHAPTER 4 Cyberwar

53 CHAPTER 5 Spammed

63 CHAPTER 6 Internet Piracy and the Culture of Free

71 CHAPTER 7 Online Criminals and Victims: The World of Cyberpolicing

79 CAREER INFORMATION

86 CHAPTER NOTES

95 GLOSSARY

99 FURTHER READING

102 INDEX

INTRODUCTION

COMPUTER FORENSICS: A DIGITAL CRIME SCENE INVESTIGATOR

After a home burglary has occurred, police detectives collect evidence of the crime so that they can identify the criminal. They might question the neighbors if they observed any suspicious activity. They look for physical evidence, such as fingerprints, footprints, or a cigarette butt. They may query workers in nearby pawn shops, or obtain a warrant to search a suspect's home for stolen goods.

All the while, the detectives must also ensure that they collect and preserve the evidence so that it can be used in court if and when the burglar is caught and brought to trial.

But what if the thief used a computer to steal money? He didn't break into the homes of his victims; he hacked into their computers. Just as a burglar might try to hide his tracks at the scene of a crime, a computer criminal might also try to hide digital evidence that could incriminate him. This poses special challenges to digital crime scene investigators; in addition to looking for fingerprints or talking to eyewitnesses, they must comb through computer files for the evidence they need to identify and convict a thief.

Initially, computer crime scene investigation (CSI) is much like any CSI. Investigators carefully document the scene, taking photos and checking for fingerprints or other physical evidence. Then, the detectives will typically seize computers, cell phones, personal digital assistants, USB drives, and tablets—any electronic device that may hold useful information—and bring them back to a government forensic laboratory for analysis.

Back at the lab, an investigator begins by making an exact duplicate of the computer's hard drive—a process called "imaging." The image is a duplicate not just of the files, but

An FBI special agent displays the world's largest English-language forum cybercriminals used to buy and sell hacked databases, malware, and other malicious products.

also of every bit stored on the drive. Every piece of data on the hard drive is preserved.

Working from the duplicate hard drive, the investigators use special software that allows them to search for and examine the contents without altering them. They can dig up passwords, email, instant messages, photographs, and the user's

internet history. Even after the user has deleted a certain file, experts can often still retrieve the data.

"Think of it as going to the library and tearing up the Dewey Decimal System cards on a particular book," said Mark Lanterman, a computer forensics expert and former member of the United States Secret Service Electronic Crimes Task Force. "The librarian may think the book is gone, but someone searching for it can still find it. Delete does not mean delete."[1]

Although cybercriminals operate with relative anonymity in the shadowy underworld of cyberspace, their crimes may leave clues that only a trained eye can identify. As more and more people and devices get connected, cybercrime touches more areas of daily life than ever. To combat the threats these unseen criminals pose, nearly every business and government sector is looking for forensic specialists who can root out digital offenders, dig up the evidence to bring them to justice, and prevent further breaches.

CHAPTER 1

CYBERCRIMINALS TAKE THE BANK FOR THE HOLIDAYS

During the bustling holiday shopping season in 2013, a simplistic malware attack stole the credit card numbers of about forty million Target shoppers.

The breach—the largest in United States retail history—happened despite a $1 million investment Target had made earlier that year to secure its transactions. They used the computer security company FireEye, whose clients included other big names invested in protecting highly sensitive information—the Pentagon and the Central Intelligence Agency (CIA)—to install malware protection. Malware (a combination of the words "malicious" and "software") is a type of software often used by cybercriminals to gain access to or damage a computer, all without the computer owner's

In 2013 Target and other major retailers became the targets of the largest retail hack in history.

knowledge. Through code, malware authors can target specific victims, whether that victim is just one person or a huge retail company and its millions of customers.

A Thief in Disguise

Target had reason to believe it was prepared to prevent cybercrime, considering its considerable investment in the malware protection and a ramped-up internal security unit.

The retail giant was partially correct in its assumption of safety. FireEye's cybersecurity system did work. A data security center in Bangalore, India, flagged the malware attacks over the weekend of November 30, 2013. The security specialists in India notified Target's headquarters in Minnesota.

FireEye's security system had a feature to stop the malware before it even got to Target's network of computers and credit card machines. However, Target turned off that feature. And, according to Target, the hackers gained access to its technology through a third-party refrigeration and heating vendor, Fazio Mechanical Services, contracted by Target for mechanical services. Though the billing and contract work transacted between Target and Fazio was conducted through a part of Target's system that's walled off from the part that handles sensitive customer data, the hackers snuck their malicious code in under the guise of a legitimate data product, associated with a known vendor. Much like a serial thief who uses wigs and disguises to prevent detection from security cameras and guards, Target's hackers found a disguise, identified entry and exit points, and slipped past the security guards.

Although Target's headquarters had been notified of the breaches, the company did not immediately act on the information. For almost two weeks, the malware authors stole tens of millions of credit card numbers and proceeded to sell them online. Target customers who had swiped anything from gift cards to debit and credit cards found their

Cyberpolitics

As the sun set on President Barack Obama's second and final term in office, the world watched as the Republican presidential nominee, real estate tycoon, and celebrity television star Donald Trump defeated his Democratic challenger—former First Lady, congresswoman, and Secretary of State Hillary Clinton.

Trump's victory was shrouded in controversy and allegations of a hacked and compromised Democratic campaign. In the months leading up to the presidential election, US intelligence indicated Russian hackers were interfering in the presidential election by targeting Democratic party members. This intelligence was backed up by the theft and subsequent leak of emails and documents belonging to members of Clinton's campaign staff, the Democratic National Committee, and other Democratic organizations. The hacked information was published on WikiLeaks, a site where anonymous sources post news leaks, classified documents, and other secret information. The leaks began during the summer of 2016 and cast a shadow of doubt over the Clinton campaign. Some contend the leaks compromised Clinton's chance for a win.

Following Trump's win, the Central Intelligence Agency investigated claims that Russian hackers were behind the Democrat breach and subsequent information leak. In December the agency announced that Russian hackers were responsible for stealing and leaking the Democrats' information in those critical pre-election days. According to the investigation, the Clinton campaign breach likely began when her campaign chair, John Podesta, received a "phishing" email that granted hackers access to his emails. Because Russian hackers had stolen emails and documents from Republicans but refrained from leaking them to the public, the CIA concluded the leak was intended to harm Clinton's campaign.[1]

In recent years, hackers from Russia and several of its neighbors have kept cybercrime investigators busy. In 2013 Ukrainian and Russian hackers stole credit card data from millions of American shoppers in an unprecedented security breach of major American retailers. Edward Snowden, a former CIA employee and government contractor, fled to Russia after he famously copied and leaked classified information. Russia granted him asylum rather than extradite him back to the United States to face criminal charges.

(continued on page 17)

US president Donald Trump has been at the center of back-and-forth accusations regarding hacking of political opponents—with Russia playing a key role.

(continued from page 15)

Russia responded to American accusations of interference in December 2016 by arresting a few citizens suspected of treason. Unfortunately, those arrests have choked the flow of Russia's cybercrime information and cooperation with the United States.[2]

Trump denies that he knew about or possibly encouraged the hack of Clinton's campaign. Russian hackers continue to target Democrats and other progressive parties. In early 2017, at least a dozen such organizations, including Pennsylvania's senate Democratic caucus, were victims of ransomware—a virus that locks a user's system or documents and holds them hostage until a ransom is paid. France and the Netherlands have pointed the finger at Russia over similar election hacks.[3]

Hackers have evolved. They've shown they can do more than steal credit card numbers. If they can disrupt an established political process, who will disrupt them?

gift card balances and bank accounts drained or their credit cards maxed out. Had Target reacted to the breaches immediately, its cybersecurity specialists could have trailed the malware authors. After all, the hackers had embedded user names and passwords directly into the malware code.

Hunting Down the Hackers

Finally, on December 12, 2013, US federal law enforcement agencies stepped in. Federal agencies had information on the stolen data and the servers—computer programs that carry out tasks for users—where the hackers were storing the stolen data.

While Target responded to customer and federal pressure to stop the theft of credit card information, the United States government's cybercrime investigators pursued the hackers who'd successfully carried out an unprecedented breach. Following a complicated web of overwhelmed proxy servers (which provide gateways between local servers and servers connected to larger networks), user names, passwords connected to video gamers, and internet protocol (IP) addresses (identifiers assigned to each computer or device), federal authorities zeroed in on Russian and Ukrainian cybercriminals they believed were responsible for all or part of the Target hacking scandal.[4] In the weeks and months to follow, other major retailers such as Home Depot and card-issuing banks such as Chase and Capitol One were hit with malware like the one that breached Target's system, indicating the malware not only worked but was shared among a network of cyber thieves.[5]

However, to date, there is no public record of the Russian and Ukrainian suspects being arrested for the massive malware attack. In early 2014, two Mexicans crossing the border into Texas were arrested when ninety fraudulent credit cards were found in their possession. Authorities believed the cards were possibly bought in connection to the card information sold by Target's hackers, but the carder—a hacker who specializes in stolen credit card information—believed to be at the center of the malware scheme seems to have fallen off the radar.[6] Andrey Hodirevski, a young Ukrainian hacker known to authorities from prior carder stings, had connections to at least one of the sites that sold the stolen credit card data. That site, rescator.cc, brazenly still operates. And though authorities have identified Rescator and other similar sites that sell stolen credit card data, some of those criminally run sites have installed their own protections, such as detecting when an undercover law enforcement agent is attempting to purchase data and infiltrate the world of the infiltrators.[7] Without definitive proof that Hodirevski is behind Rescator, and that his known or assumed associates are behind that site and others that sell credit card information, law enforcement agencies around the globe labor to pinpoint cybercriminals suspected of one of the worst security breaches in retail history. And while they labor to draw definitive lines between suspects and criminal sites, they must also continue trying to catch these underworld thieves in the act. Sites that sold credit card data used to be public, for the most part. As cybercriminals continue to learn from their mistakes, however, users of stolen credit card sites must now have log-in credentials to purchase credit card information and filter credit card data by region to escape detection. For instance, a credit or debit card belonging to a California resident

Cybercriminals devote their time not only to theft of stolen data but also to thwarting investigators trying to shut them down.

being used in New York or abroad would raise a red flag for most banks and credit card companies and even result in freezing the account while the activity is verified with the account owner. Many banks and credit card companies now ask their customers to identify authorized card users and specific dates and places a card might be used away from home in order to tailor fraud detection and prevention. By allowing customers of stolen card data to filter by region, cybercriminals undermine the systems banks and credit card companies have in place to secure customer data. Mark Lanterman obtained credentials for black-market credit card information sites after years undercover on underworld sites.

"You just hang out," Lanterman told Bloomberg in 2014. "Eventually they just think you're the same kind of scumbag they are and say, 'Yep, here's your login.'"[8]

Now that the fraudsters have installed protections against the fraud detectors, a new wave of cybercrime investigators is needed: a generation that grew up online, knows the stakes, and is ready to play the long game. Because criminals are looking for customers and cohorts with an established history of online criminal activity, crime fighters must be in for the long haul and know how to spring a trap that can ensnare a vast network of criminals who operate in the darkest corner of the underworld of crime: online.

CHAPTER 2

THE EARLY DAYS OF CYBERCRIME

In the decades leading up to personal computers and the internet, computers were primarily owned by large companies, universities, and government agencies. These computers, called mainframes, took up entire rooms and were expensive (in 1960, a typical IBM mainframe cost several million dollars[1]). Cards punched with holes were read by the computers, and users often waited hours, if not days, for the data results. Mainframe computers were not networked with any other computers, and only a select group of people in an organization had direct access to them. So only a few insiders were in any position to commit computer crimes, and these crimes stayed within their own organizations.

This 1950 photo shows an early mainframe computer, described by creators as an efficient way to design and construct missiles, ships, and submarines.

Phreaking: The Precursor to Hacking

The underground computer culture that would eventually give rise to both widespread innovation and cybercrime began quite innocently. In 1957 an eight-year-old boy discovered that when he whistled the E note above middle C into a telephone, the system's computers gave him control of a line that allowed him to make free long-distance phone calls. Because the boy, Joe Engressia, had perfect pitch, he could create the tone any time, just by whistling. He wasn't as interested in making free long-distance calls—although he did do that—as he was in learning the ins and outs of the phone system. Over the following years, he became better at controlling the phone system, and he shared his knowledge with others. The phone phreaks (a combination of "phone" and "freaks") realized that what they were really doing was probing a very large and complex computer system. The early phone phreaks were stealing services from the telephone company, but they did not think of themselves as thieves. In a later interview with *Esquire* magazine, Engressia said that he phreaked "for the pleasure of pure knowledge. There's something beautiful about the system when you know it intimately."[2]

"It was the only game in town if you wanted to play with a computer," said phreaking expert Phil Lapsley.[3] The police and FBI investigated many phone phreaks; some were arrested, convicted, and sent to prison. Engressia was eventually arrested for theft of services, but his jail sentence was suspended on the condition that he never phreak again. Eventually, phone phreaking died out as the telephone companies improved and secured their call-switching systems.

Early hackers were primarily interested in understanding and manipulating a complex computer system. The original hackers were a group of Massachusetts Institute of Technology (MIT) students who, in the late 1950s and early 1960s, managed to gain access to the university's mainframe computers.

Joe Engressia, pictured here in 1968, was an early phone phreak who discovered that whistling a certain tone into the telephone receiver granted him free long distance.

How Cybercriminals Do What They Do

Like traditional crooks, cybercriminals steal, murder, and traffic in illegal goods and information. What sets them apart are the ways in which the crimes are committed. Whereas traditional gangsters such as Al Capone relied upon guns, cybercriminals use computers as weapons. (One can only imagine what Capone, the notorious 1920s-era Chicago gangster, would have done with computer technology!) According to the US Department of Justice, computers can play three distinct roles in criminal cases.[4]

- A computer or computer network can be the target of a crime. Commonly, computer crimes occur when hackers gain unauthorized access to a computer system to steal credit or debit card numbers or other personal information. Hackers can breach corporate computers to steal and duplicate copyrighted software programs to sell on the black market or to steal valuable company secrets. Infecting computers or networks with malware such as worms and viruses is another type of computer-targeted crime.

- Computers can be used to help commit a crime. Many traditional crimes can be committed online. A dealer who sells illegal drugs through email or websites rather than on a street corner is using the computer as a tool to commit the crime. Computers can be used to commit fraud (a type of theft in which someone is tricked into giving away something of value), distribute child pornography, or harass or threaten people (cyberstalking).
- Computers can play a minor role in the offense of the crime, although they may be very important in investigating and prosecuting a crime. For example, say a woman poisons her husband. After the murder, computer forensics experts on the police force examine the woman's computer. They find emails between the woman and a friend in which they plot her husband's death; her browser history shows that she had done research on how to poison someone. In this case, the computer was an important piece of evidence requiring the expertise of a computer forensics expert.

Of course, in any given crime, computers may play more than one of these roles.

These students were interested in using computers both to solve hard problems and to carry out clever but harmless pranks. These white hat (a term borrowed from old Western movies, in which the good guys wore white hats, while the bad guys wore black hats) hackers had developed a "philosophy, an ethic, and a dream," as described by Steven Levy in his book *Hackers*. "To a hacker, a closed door is an insult, and a locked door is an outrage . . . [H]ackers believe people should be allowed access to files or tools which might promote the hacker quest to find out and improve the way the world works."[5] The hacking culture spread to other universities, with hackers exploring the growing number of computer systems and writing innovative new programs. They shared what they created and learned.

A Spreading Phenomenon

Two developments brought hacking to a wider audience. The first was the internet. It might seem hard to imagine a time when you couldn't just turn on your computer, phone, or tablet and check your Facebook, but the internet is younger than you might think. It began in 1969 as a research project funded by the US Department of Defense. The goal of the project, called the Advanced Research Projects Agency Network (ARPANET), was to provide a way for a network of computers to communicate even if some of the sites were destroyed by a nuclear attack. ARPANET linked computers of universities, research centers, government agencies, and defense contractors. ARPANET and other computer networks were the forerunners of the internet. Over the next few decades, the internet expanded and became open to private companies. It became much easier to use, and by 1998 there were 150 million people online.[6]

The rise of personal computers brought the internet to ordinary people who weren't necessarily computer whizzes. The first personal computers came on the market in 1977, and suddenly the power of the internet landed on the desktops of the masses. As an early promotional video for the Apple II computer put it, "We build a device that gives people the same power over information that large corporations and the government have over people."[7]

Personal computers opened the world of computer systems to a whole new generation of hackers with little computer experience. Malicious hackers gained national attention in 1983, when a group of young men from the Milwaukee, Wisconsin, area used their personal computers and dial-up modems to hack into more than sixty high-profile computer systems. Their targets included a nuclear weapons laboratory in Los Alamos, New Mexico, and a large cancer hospital in New York City.

The half-dozen young men, ranging in age from sixteen to twenty-two, used common or default passwords and security holes to hack into the

The rise of personal computers in the 1970s, such as this early Apple II, brought everyday people into the use of computers. Those early computers spawned an array of electronic devices that now practically manage our lives for us.

computers. As far as they were concerned, they were just engaged in a little harmless snooping. The cancer hospital, which found that the hackers had deleted more than $1,500 worth of billing records, thought otherwise. The FBI agreed. Two of the six were prosecuted; the four who were not had to pay for the damages and agree not to engage in hacking again.[8] One of the hackers said that the group was inspired by the 1983 movie *War Games,* in which a teenager hacks into a military network as a prank. In the movie, the teen's escapade is nearly disastrous when he comes close to launching a nuclear missile and starting World War III.

By 1984 one hacker-turned-FBI-informant called hacking "an epidemic. In practically every upper-middle class high school this is going on. I know of a high-school computer class in the north Dallas suburbs where the kids are trying everything they can think of to get into the CIA computers." The informant estimated that 75 percent of criminal hackers were teenagers and the other 25 percent were adults using teenagers to do their dirty work for them. "There are no foreign agents or organized crime yet, but it's inevitable," he added. "I believe there are some people out there now with possible organized-crime connections."[9]

The informant was right on target.

CHAPTER 3

THE INTERNET OF THINGS

Most of us use tablets, cell phones, laptops, desktop computers, video game consoles, and even home security systems that all rely at least in part on one thing: the internet. This congregation of internet-adherent devices has created what some call "the internet of things."

As one technology writer explained, the ever-expanding use and availability of the internet means anything with "an on and off switch to the internet" can, and in the future probably will, be connected to other devices with internet connection capability. These machines can then talk to each other through the data and code embedded in the software and hardware that makes them function. Many technologists see unlimited potential in the possibility of such enhanced communication between machines, particularly in the areas of added efficiency and convenience.[1] Already, smartphones can be used to control the temperature in someone's home when he or she isn't even home. Private security systems can be armed or disarmed from a smartphone or computer when, again, the person who lives in that home isn't even there.

All this connectivity sounds great. But when interconnectedness expands, so do the vulnerabilities of the devices and network that create the web of connectivity.

Essentially, the idea is that one home or centralized network is running any number of internet-using devices at one time. For instance, the installer of a home security system in the Dallas suburbs might access and share the home network name and password of a customer to individuals around the globe. This is possible because he had access to that information while installing a system that depends on the internet to access information. Through the security system set up, the installer can find out sensitive information such as the names of the homeowners buying and installing the product; their phone numbers and address; the names and contact information of the customers' "in case of emergency" contacts; the password the customers chose to communicate ownership of their security system with the security company; their Wi-Fi passwords; and what internet-using equipment their home contains: video game systems, AppleTV, cell phones, computers—the list goes on.

One is never enough. Laptops, smartphones, tablets, Bluetooth devices, and web-connected homes have given rise to "the internet of things."

Much of the data and personal information stored on all our interconnected devices is consolidated in one place, such as a home network or a data plan. It's like a human skeleton. And once one arm is broken, the rest of the body is weakened—an unhappy circumstance when virus writers are looking for a way into a home or business network. The more devices you add to a network, the more vulnerabilities cybercriminals can find. Law enforcement and cybercrime investigators must deploy every available technology to combat the underworld criminals looking for gaps in the system.

"Virus writers seem emboldened by technology and enjoy the thrill of watching the damage they reap," said US attorney Christopher J. Christie. "But . . . [l]aw enforcement can employ technology too and track down virus writers and hackers through the electronic fingerprints they invariably leave behind."[2]

We've seen how viruses such as malware can wreak havoc on victims and networks worldwide. Personal and banking information, contacts, credit card numbers, our very identities: today's cybercriminals can find it all. And all of it is for sale.

Rise of the Botnet

Today's virus writers are interested in much more than wreaking havoc on computer networks. They want our money—and they're using our computers to get it.

Primarily through malware- or virus-infected hyperlinks, attachments, or downloads, users who click the links, open the attachments, or download something from an email or site unknowingly download a nasty piece of software called a bot.

You've got a virus! Armies of computers that have been taken over by criminals work tirelessly on behalf of virus writers looking to gain access to your system.

Once a computer is infected with a bot, it joins an army of infected "zombie" PCs called a botnet. From its new home, the bot (short for "robot") sends a message to its command server: "Here I am. What do you want me to do, master?" The botnet owners, or "bot herders," use the zombie computers to perform criminal activity—all without the knowledge of the owners of the computers. Botnets can send spam emails, steal data at banking and shopping websites, bombard sites in an effort to shut them down, or spread new infections. They may even pose a threat to national security.

Botnets are a huge problem. Computer security expert Rick Wesson says that on any given day, 40 percent of the eight hundred million computers connected to the internet are part of one or more botnets.[3] Rival online gangs wage a virtual turf war over the largest botnets. The larger the army of zombie computers, the more money spammers and hackers will pay to use them. In 2015 the FBI, the US Department of Justice, the British government, Europol, and private companies such as Dell took on a network of malware authors deploying code through enslaved bot computers. The hackers behind the bot operation stole at least ten million dollars from people in the United States alone. The hackers obtained banking information by stealing computer users' passwords and signing in to bank accounts. Andrey Ghinkul, believed to be at the center of the hacking and botnet ring, was arrested in Cyprus

During a 2010 conference in Washington, DC, Rick Wesson briefs a group of business, political, and academic leaders on the critical issues facing cybersecurity.

Protect Your Computer from Bot Herders

Here are some tips for keeping your computer safe from cyber crooks:

1. Use antivirus and anti-spyware software and keep it up to date.
2. Set your operating system to download and install security patches automatically.
3. Be cautious about opening attachments or downloading files from emails you receive. Don't open an email attachment, even if it looks like it's from a friend, unless you're expecting it or know what it contains.
4. Use a firewall to protect your computer from hacking attacks while it is connected to the internet. A firewall is software or hardware designed to block malicious hackers from gaining access to your computer.
5. Turn off your computer when you are not using it.
6. Download free software only from sites you know and trust.
7. Delete emails that are obviously spam without opening them. Do not click on suspicious links in emails.

in late 2015. Money he and his cohorts stole was allegedly sent back to bank accounts in Belarus and Ukraine. Experts at Dell SecureWorks were among the first to identify the thefts and breaches, and after the go-ahead from the authorities, set to work taking down the botnet. Once they had control of the botnet, the Shadowserver Foundation, a group of hackers that works to make the internet safer for users, took control of the botnet.

Unfortunately, only the botnet network was dismantled. The malware still exists. The 2015 case focused mostly on the malware called Dridex that was infecting computers and creating botnets all around the globe.

"It's not over. It's not even close to over," Kevin Epstein, a researcher at security firm Proofpoint, told CNN's tech division. "Dridex is back with a vengeance. If you're selling drugs and someone takes out your distributor, does it take the drugs off the street?"[4]

In February 2017, Ghinkul pleaded guilty to his part of the international theft ring, including the one million dollars he tried but failed to steal from a school district in Pennsylvania. The charges he pleaded guilty to are federal, and he could face up to five years in prison and extradition back home to the Republic of Moldova.[5]

Devious Deeds via DDoS

Botnets aren't always used to steal money or data. Sometimes they're used by hackers to blackmail, exact revenge, or simply to prove a point. Hackers in those scenarios might use a botnet herd to deploy a distributed denial of service (DDoS) attack. DDoS attacks intentionally paralyze a computer network by flooding it with data from multiple IP addresses. Because of the rise of the internet of things, hackers can use any number or combination of internet-connected devices to shut down a site or entire network.

In mid-September 2016, cybersecurity investigative reporter Brian Krebs wrote a series about DDoS-for-hire services. For individuals or entities without the capability or skills to deploy a DDoS attack, DDoS-for-hire services will deploy one for a fee. The series, chronicled on Krebs's site, krebsonsecurity.com, coincided with the arrests of two men he'd named as part of a DDoS-for-hire service. On September 20, 2016, his site was hit with a DDoS attack—but successfully repelled by Akamai, the content delivery network Krebs employs to protect his site from such attacks. Akamai's analysts told Krebs the attempted attack on his site was almost double the largest DDoS attack they'd previously seen, and "among the biggest assaults the Internet has ever witnessed."

Though Krebs does not definitively say the attempted attack was hacker revenge for his DDoS series and the arrest of DDos-for-hire hackers, he does write, "it seems likely related."[6]

Akamai's Network Operations Command Center helped repel a DDoS attack aimed at Brian Krebs following an exposé the writer posted about DDoS-for-hire hackers.

Sometimes money is the motivation for a DDoS attack. Hackers are increasingly targeting financial institutions with DDoS attacks to extort payment, typically through Bitcoin. A cybercriminal group called DD4BC (DDoS for Bitcoin) has been hitting banks, brokerages, and automated clearing houses in Europe, Australia, and the United States since 2015.[7] Europol arrested two suspected members of DD4BC in January 2016, but the war is far from over.

CHAPTER 4

CYBERWAR

In 2010 someone at a nuclear power plant in Iran plugged a USB flash drive into one of the facility's computers. That seemingly innocent action launched what some have called the world's first known cybermissile, a weapon designed to seek out and destroy a real-world target.

The flash drive was infected with a computer worm called Stuxnet (the name comes from some keywords in the software). The worm instantly loaded itself onto the computer and searched for a specialized software program called WinCC. This program is used to control industrial equipment used to run factories, chemical and power plants, and electric power grids all over the world. When the worm found WinCC running, it logged in, created a secret "back door" to the internet, and contacted a server in Malaysia for instructions. The back door allowed the mysterious attackers to harvest data about the system. Worse, the attackers could now assume control of critical systems such as valves, pumps, motors, and alarms

CYBERSTORM

In early 2016, a diverse group of hackers distributed malware in the United States, resulting in crippling effects in critical infrastructure sectors. In the end, federal agencies, commercial retailers, law enforcement and intelligence agencies, state and international governments, health care and public affairs organizations, and information technology companies were embroiled in a massive cyberattack on the United States.

The attack lasted four days but did little damage. It was only a cybersecurity drill, sponsored by the Department of Homeland Security (DHS), to test the nation's ability to respond to a cyberattack. The drill, called Cyber Storm V (four previous cybersecurity drills tested the nation's cybersecurity, each with different partnerships and goals), gave the government a chance to see how ready it was to protect itself against cyberwarfare. After retailer breaches such as those that stole millions of credit card information from stores such as Target in 2013, the government drill brought in multiple retailers.

"We're looking to find the failure points, to raise the bar in every scenario," Gregory Touhill, a Department of Homeland Security deputy assistant secretary, said.[1]

in the plant. They could even switch off safety systems if they wanted. Stuxnet spread from machine to machine in the power plant's network.

Unearthing the Worm

A computer security firm detected Stuxnet in June 2010. By August of that year, the malware had infected forty-five thousand computers, 60 percent of them in Iran. By February 2017, malware related to Stuxnet infected more than one hundred banks in forty countries around the globe. Twenty-one of

Employees work at the Bushehr nuclear power plant in Iran. Though damage was minimal, a Western alliance was behind the 2010 Stuxnet worm attack on the plant.

those cases were in the United States.[2] Although many of those computers were not running the targeted software, it wormed its way into fifteen industrial plants using WinCC around the world. "Stuxnet is a 100 percent-directed cyber-attack aimed at destroying an industrial process in the physical world," said Ralph Langner, a German cybersecurity researcher who studied the malware. "The whole attack is not at all about stealing data but about manipulation of a specific industrial process at a specific moment in time."[3]

What was the target of the Stuxnet worm—and who was behind it? Given that most of the affected computers were in Iran, experts believed Stuxnet's goal was to destroy Iran's nuclear plants. The Iranian government said Stuxnet did not do major damage to the power plant and other nuclear facilities in the country, but its derivatives did eventually inflict extensive damage. Though Iran insists its nuclear program is for peaceful purposes only, much of the world believes that it is intent upon developing nuclear weapons.

Stuxnet was so complex and sophisticated that experts believed it was created by a government organization to prevent Iran from developing a nuclear weapon. They were correct. Stuxnet was part of an Israeli-United States program: Operation Olympic Games.

Experts worried Stuxnet would be used as a blueprint for copycat cyberwarriors.

They were right to be worried. The worm got away from the operation after Israel altered a version of Stuxnet. Iran built its own cyberweapons in response and ramped up its nuclear efforts. In 2014 the United States launched a similar attack against North Korea with similar goals: to stunt nuclear production. The United States failed in its attempt.[4]

Old Rivalries Resurface

In centuries past, countries engaged in massive physical battles that claimed millions of lives, in everything from arm-to-arm combat to trench warfare to dropping atomic bombs. Between 1947 and 1991, the United States and its allies engaged in a continuous campaign against the Soviet Union—Russia and its satellite states—during a conflict called the Cold War. Named "Cold" because no direct large-scale battles took place, this war is perhaps best known for the nuclear arms race between the United States and Russia. With the Soviet Union and its communist allies strictly isolated from the rest of the world, government and military agencies feverishly attempted to gather intelligence in the days before information could be sent over continents and oceans with the single click of a mouse.

Fearing nuclear attacks, Cold War enemies raced to discover and outdo each other's military, scientific, and growing technological advances.[5] Nations

The Cyber Cold War

The 2016 United States presidential election proved foreign cybercriminals have the mettle to disrupt the country's established democratic process. Because the cyberattacks that shrouded the 2016 presidential election largely originated in Russia, some experts are hailing the attacks as signs of the Cyber Cold War.

The first Cold War, waged primarily between the United States and Russia, was notable for its arms race, spies, and fears over nuclear war. The Cyber Cold War parallels the first Cold War in that, once again, the United States and Russia are on opposing sides. Technology, however, has updated the ways in which war works and looks. The ability to infiltrate or debilitate an enemy from a computer halfway around the globe has virtually eliminated the need for human spies or military combatants. Rather than threatening each other with nuclear warfare, Cyber Cold War battles are waged online, as evidenced by the damage Russian hackers caused during the 2016 presidential election. In its simplest definition, war appears to have revisited the old Cold War enemies.

"There's something unsettling about calling this a war. But it's frivolous to ignore this," said Laura Galante, intelligence director at FireEye, to CNN Tech in January 2017. "The Russians get it right, and they're beating the U.S."[6]

Shot Grable was one of eleven nuclear test shots in 1953 in Nevada. During the Cold War, the Americans and Soviets raced to outdo each other's nuclear capabilities.

placed spies in enemy territory and gathered intelligence through covert and often dangerous operations, including turning government agents against their home nations and squeezing them for classified information. However, as the Cold War progressed into the 1980s, so did technologies such as desktop computers. Use of computers and portable storage devices such as floppy disks—thin, flexible magnetic storage disks once commonly used to save information from computers—became more common. Though the technology was nowhere near as sophisticated as what we know and use today, Cold War enemies and spies vied for digital intelligence understood by few people. The need for government and military personnel who had information technology expertise skyrocketed; enemy operations scripted in computer code on a floppy disk would have meant little or nothing to the average Cold War–era intelligence officer. Spies were no longer just shadowy agents in disguise. Computers and developments such as ARPANET introduced the need for teams of information technology experts to

Though unsophisticated compared to current technologies, the floppy disk made data and information portable.

crack codes and develop and understand complex software. Accordingly, the demand for experts who could help their countries protect their digital assets and information increased.[7]

Fast forward to the twenty-first century. The main fear that motivated Cold War spies is what motivated Stuxnet: nuclear warfare. How nations respond to that fear today looks completely different, however. The spy games that occupied governments during the forty-four years of the Cold War have adapted to newly available technologies, and Stuxnet is proof. Warfare has moved to cyberspace. Major nations are racing to find new ways to protect computer networks—and the critical structures and facilities they control—from their enemies.

CHAPTER 5

SPAMMED

For nearly twenty years, almost anyone with an email address has received an odd email from an unknown sender with a strange request. The African prince who promises part of his fortune to those who send him money is perhaps the most well-known of all the spam email scams that have plagued email users since the internet became a global commodity. It's called an "advance fee" scam, or 419 scam (after Article 419 of Nigeria's criminal code which focuses on fraud), and of course, the prince's rescuers never see a return on their investment in the unfortunate royal.

The Man Behind the Spam

The phony African prince scam worked on enough email recipients that one spammer, Okpako Mike Diamreyan (aka Prince Nana Kamokai, but in reality a Nigerian citizen who moved to the United States in 2008 after marrying an American) managed to bilk

The number 419 is given to common internet scams originating from Africa, home of the disenfranchised African prince scam.

$1.3 million from sixty-one victims, most of them senior citizens. Prince Nana Kamokai was only one of the aliases and email only one of the methods, he used to steal money from trusting victims, but the email spam was the most effective way to reach a large audience.

Diamreyan came to the attention of the US Defense Criminal Investigative Service. Based on phone and email records provided by victims of the scam, investigators zeroed in on Diamreyan. In July 2009, he was found with cell phones, SIM cards, and a flash drive—and enough evidence for a search warrant for his apartment in Massachusetts. Email and phone records from the searches tied Diamreyan solidly to the scams.

In 2010 Diamreyan was sentenced to more than twelve years in federal prison and ordered to pay his victims more than $1 million.

Many people have a hard time believing anyone would fall for such a scam, but many—especially senior citizens who did not grow up with the internet—are deceived by them. The US Secret Service estimates that advance fee fraud schemes like Diamreyan's steal hundreds of millions of dollars each year.[1] If something sounds too good to be true, it probably is!

Baiting, Hooking, and Kidnapping Your Data

As the public becomes warier of scams as blatant as the troubled African prince, cybercriminals are using other spamlike techniques to obtain victims' personal and financial information. One way they do this is called "phishing," a practice cybercriminals use to attack computers with malicious software. ("Phishing" is a combination of "phreaking" and "fishing".) Phishers pose as legitimate companies or contacts via email, text, or pop-up messages.[2] For instance, someone who uses Microsoft Office may receive an email reporting a problem with his or her software from someone who claims to work at Microsoft. The email looks legitimate, so the user takes the bait and gives up his or her Microsoft Office credentials. Once the hacker has that information, he or she can access anything from personal information to banking information. The hacker posing as Microsoft tech support may also provide links to

Young men deploy computer scams in an internet café in Ghana. Limited opportunities for legitimate work drive many young people to turn to fraud for income.

other sites in the fraudulent email; once a user clicks that link, they unwittingly allow viruses or malware onto their machine.[3] Some phishers will text, knowing that mobile devices often contain fewer security features than standard computers and are therefore more easily hacked.[4]

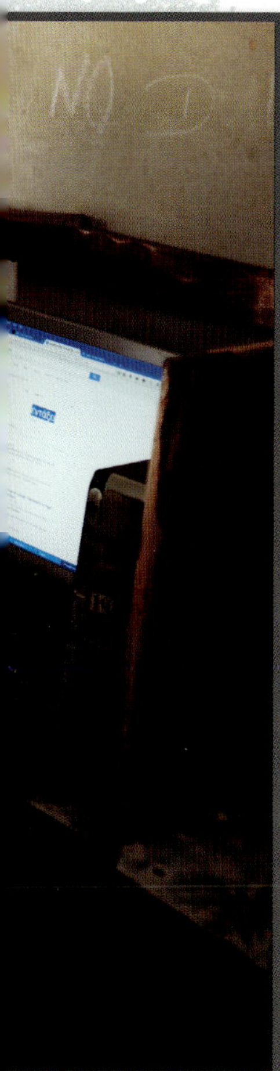

As cybercriminals such as phishers find new ways to install malicious software on our personal, school, or work computers, they're also devising new ways of handling our information after they gain access.

While scams such as the African prince tended to target individuals, modern hackers and cybercriminals have bigger fish to fry: big companies that hold large amounts of sensitive data.

To catch the big fish, one of the more recent cybercrime developments is ransomware. Ransomware can victimize individuals, but it's large companies that hackers are after with this type of attack—because it's through big companies that hackers will get paid.

Ransomware delivers malicious software to devices and their networks via a Trojan horse or through a network vulnerability and running a payload—the part of a worm, virus, or malware that carries out a specific nefarious task, such as sending spam

GOING PHISHING

1. Potential victims receive an email that appears to come from a bank, internet service provider, or other well-known or reputable agency.
2. The email message describes an urgent reason why the recipients must verify or resubmit passwords or other confidential information by clicking on a link embedded in the message. Facebook scams originate with an invitation from a "friend" to click on a link to see a funny video.
3. Clicking on the link will take the victims to a website that appears to be legitimate, but which was actually set up by the scammer.
4. Once at the website, the victims are asked to provide passwords, Social Security numbers, bank account numbers, or other identification that might be useful.
5. If the victims provide the information, the scammers can take over their email accounts or other personal accounts. If you suspect an email or website is fraudulent, do not reply or provide any information!

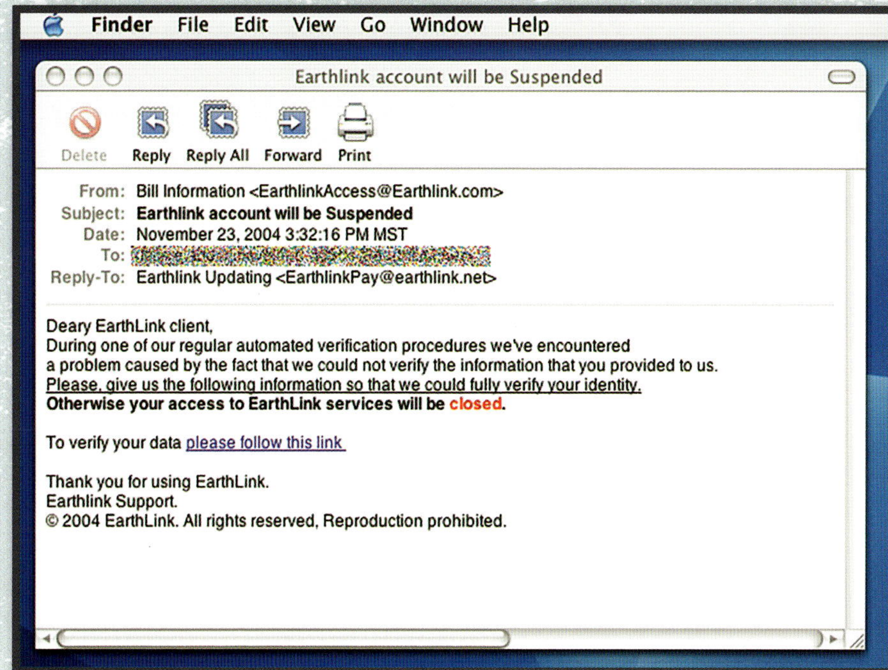

A phishing email poses as a legitimate customer support email, luring the customer into opening malicious files or links that steal information from his or her device.

or deleting or encrypting data. Some victims of ransomware will find their screens or systems locked or restricted until the victims pay the ransom, usually via hard to trace payment systems such as wire transfers or the digital currency Bitcoin, to regain access to their data and systems. Other victims may find themselves on the receiving end of more sophisticated ransomware that uses encryption to lock files or systems until the ransom payment is made. The hackers then provide a key to unlock the encrypted information.[5] Even after

Protect Yourself from Email Scams

- Use a strong, unique password for each online account. Passwords should mix special characters ($, ?, or &, for example), numbers, and uppercase and lowercase letters.
- Use a phishing filter on your computer. Many current web browsers have them built-in or offer them as plug-ins.
- Never follow a link to an important site from an email message—always enter the web address manually. If you hover your cursor over the link and see a web address that is different from the one printed in the message, don't even bother going there at all.
- If you know that someone has hacked into your email account, change your password immediately. Call your internet service provider if you've been locked out of your account.
- If you discover that a fake email has gone out under your name, notify your contacts and tell them to ignore it.
- Tell a parent or guardian about any scams you encounter. They can report them to the internet Crime Complaint Center (www.ic3.gov) and the Federal Trade Commission (www.ftc.gov).

paying the ransom, victims—which can range from one individual to huge corporations—may never again see all or some of their data, or may find their sensitive information published by the ransomware author. For corporations that rely on computers and networks to handle sensitive information such as new product plans, customer data, and payment information, unpaid ransoms could mean the release of trade secrets and customer information. In the case of hospitals or insurance companies, an unpaid ransom could mean the loss and public release of patient health information—a devastating result for patients and doctors who rely on a hospital's systems to access, record, and track patient health care needs.[6]

Ransomware is on the rise, with hundreds of thousands of types of ransomware in circulation, and earning cyber kidnappers quite a lot of money. Just like a parent whose child has been kidnapped, ransomware victims are showing how desperate they are to get their information and systems back: one type of ransomware, CryptoWall, earned hackers $325 million in ransom payments in 2015 alone.[7]

While desperate victims such as hospitals often pay to get their information and systems back, experts advise against paying ransomware authors. Payment emboldens ransomware authors to continue their work. Instead, experts caution individuals and companies to train themselves to detect anything suspicious. This includes detecting unusual emails, pop-ups, attachments, and other ways viruses find

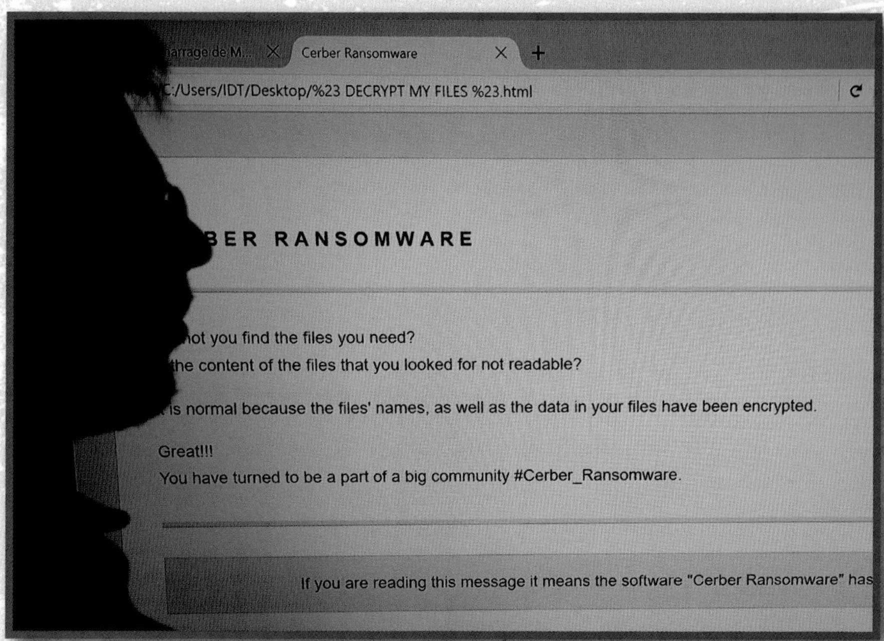

At a high-security lab, researchers for the National Institute for Research in Computer Science and Automation examine ransomware—one of the most dangerous computer scams on the market.

their way onto our devices and refraining from taking the bait. Experts advise individuals and companies to back up all their information on drives or servers rather than storing everything on devices alone. Individuals and companies also need to keep up with threats by keeping their security measures up to date and perhaps even enhancing them to detect ransomware.[8] Ransomware has become a top priority for investigative agencies such as the FBI, the lead federal agency for investigating cyberattacks by criminals domestic and abroad.[9]

CHAPTER 6

INTERNET PIRACY AND THE CULTURE OF FREE

For nearly ten months, millions of fans worldwide anxiously awaited the April 24, 2016, season six premiere of the HBO mega-hit *Game of Thrones*. The fate of several main characters was left teetering with the previous season's final episode. The internet was aflame with theories and the lament of fans who missed their favorite show.

Some fans couldn't wait.

Digital Millennium Copyright Act Thwarts "Throne" Piracy

At least one million people watched pirated copies of the show's season six premiere. The year before, the show's season five premiere was ultimately downloaded, illegally, ten million

Through torrent sites, the HBO megahit *Game of Thrones* has been illegally downloaded millions of times by anxious fans—in violation of federal law.

times.[1] This astounding number of illicit downloads was accompanied by another wrinkle: the first four episodes of the show were leaked before airing.

The network believed the episodes leaked from within a group HBO approved for previewing and review, like television critics.

The massive response among fans and distributers of pirated content proves piracy is not only a widespread problem, but one that may never be stopped.

"Piracy is a tidal wave that cannot be controlled, only managed. There is a culture of 'free' where many people believe that it is acceptable to pirate these TV shows if they don't have access to them through legal means," said Rory O'Connor, vice president of services for digital platform security company Irdeto.[2]

To warn pirates that the network was onto them, in 2016 HBO enlisted the help of internet service providers worldwide to identify the IP addresses of subscribers who had illegally downloaded content. Once identified, the subscribers received warning letters reminding them HBO owns the copyright and exclusive rights to *Game of Thrones*. The network also sent warning letters to torrent sites, where illegal downloads are often made available. Often within minutes of receipt of HBO's letter, torrent sites removed HBO's content to comply with the Digital Millennium Copyright Act (DMCA), a federal US copyright law.[3]

The Pirate Bay is a popular torrent site that allows users to illegally download and distribute music, movies, games, and other copyrighted work.

Relatively speaking, HBO was kind to the recipients of its warning letters, considering the DMCA permits copyright holders—such as television networks—to bring violators to court and demand damages.

The DMCA criminalizes illicit file sharing and the creation and sharing of technology designed to go around legal means of obtaining content. Copyright owners can press charges in both civil and criminal

WHAT IS COPYRIGHT?

Whenever you write a poem or paint a picture, you own the copyright to your work. This means that, as the creator of the work, you have the right to make and distribute copies of your work, to perform or display your work in public, and to modify or adapt your work. If somebody else wants to use your copyrighted work in any of these ways, the law says that they must first get permission from you, as it is your intellectual property. If you copy or download copyrighted music, software, movies, or e-books from the internet without paying for the works or getting permission from the creator of the works, you are committing copyright infringement. And that is against the law!

Under the current law, copyright protection of a work continues until seventy years after the death of the author or artist. When the term of copyright is finished, the work falls into the public domain. Anyone is free to make copies of Jane Austen's *Pride and Prejudice,* for example, but you could not legally make copies of Seth Grahame-Smith's 2009 mashup, *Pride and Prejudice and Zombies.*

courts. Civil penalties for DMCA violations can pay up to $2,500 per violation, or up to $25,000 in statutory damages. Copyright owners may also request the recovery of any profits the violators made, and repeat offenders can face triple damages if they repeat a DMCA violation. Criminal penalties for DMCA violations face larger fines and prison time. The DMCA defines "criminal violation" as when someone knowingly violates the law for commercial or financial gain, such as selling pirated copies of shows, movies, or other copyrighted material. Criminal violators face up to $500,000 in fines, up to five years in jail, or both a fine and jail for a first offense. Repeat offenders may face ten years in prison, up to $1 million in fines, or both.[4]

Pirates: Everywhere, Everything, Everyone

In February 2017, the New Zealand high court decided a notorious internet pirate and New Zealand resident would be extradited to the United States to face internet piracy scam charges.[5]

The pirate, who goes by Kim Dotcom, founded Megaupload, where content was allegedly made available despite copyright infringements. The pirate has described himself as an "internet freedom fighter," making him a member of a larger movement of internet lurkers who believe in a "culture of free." Members of this movement believe content, especially creative content such as music or movies,

Kim Dotcom (pictured here in New Zealand in 2014) was a longtime source of pirated work. Members paid a fee to access copyrighted material. Dotcom has been embroiled in legal fights for years.

should be made available to large audiences for free.[6]

The United States, most other countries, and the international crime-fighting organization Interpol largely disagree with the "culture of free" ideology. Piracy is technically a crime that potentially violates any nation's laws regarding theft. And because this type of theft can take place anywhere a pirate can find an internet connection, criminal investigators often find themselves working with their international counterparts to take down pirates and piracy sites. In Dotcom's case, New Zealand authorities raided the pirate's mansion in 2012, seizing 135 electronic items such as laptops, computers, hard drives, flash drives, and servers as evidence.[7] The FBI shut down Dotcom's site and requested he be extradited to the United States to face charges, claiming Megaupload earned more than $175 million in criminal proceeds and cost copyright owners more than $500 million. After five years of legal appeals and continued US pursuit of the criminal, Dotcom faces thirteen criminal charges, including copyright infringement, money laundering, and wire fraud. He faces up to twenty years in jail if convicted in the United States.[8]

With an expanding and international group touting the "culture of free" and the many ways internet pirates can carry out their trade, cybercrime fighters remain vigilant and rely on cooperation from international agencies and other countries to assure justice is served—just as any thief should expect.

CHAPTER 7

ONLINE CRIMINALS AND VICTIMS: THE WORLD OF CYBERPOLICING

In Pittsburgh, after dinner on New Year's Day 2002, thirteen-year-old Alicia Kozakiewicz excused herself from the table and went to her room. She promised to come back for dessert. When her parents checked her room around 6:00 p.m., she was gone. There was no note or sign of forced entry. Despite the cold weather, her coat was in her closet.

The police interviewed Alicia's friends and family, while neighbors searched the area. There was not a trace of the girl. FBI special agent Denise Holtz, who specialized in crimes against children, arrived on the scene late the next day. When Holtz learned Alicia spent a lot of time online, she had a feeling that the key to the girl's disappearance might be on her computer.

The clock was ticking. If a killer had abducted Alicia—and Holtz had no reason to believe otherwise—her chances of survival diminished with each passing hour.[1] Tony Pallone, an FBI computer forensic specialist, searched Alicia's computer for clues. He copied Alicia's hard drive to his computer and ran a program to analyze its contents. A software program allowed him to examine all her files, including those she'd deleted. He looked through her chat room activity, and noted that she chatted frequently with someone who went by the screen name "dcdude" (this and the following screen name of Alicia's kidnapper have been changed). And there the trail ended. Pallone could find no references to "dcdude" anywhere else on the internet. By the evening of January 3, Alicia's parents began to think they'd never see their daughter alive.

An Anonymous Tip

But then investigators got a break in the high-profile case. An anonymous man from Tampa told the FBI a man he knew as "Scott," who used the screen name "madman" in a chat room, claimed to have captured a teenage girl from Pittsburgh and taken her to his northern Virginia home. When Scott posted a video of a crying girl chained to a wall, the Tampa man matched her to a photo of Alicia in a newspaper.

Posing as a teenage girl, a cybercrime investigator in Florida logs into a chat room to monitor the activity of cyberpredators. Sting operations like this have led to the capture of many criminals.

Pallone and his colleagues searched chat rooms to find "madman." They found his Yahoo! chat profile and saw he'd listed other online aliases, including "dcdude." They had their man, but not his identity or location. Yahoo! provided the user's IP address. This told agents the country, state, city, and zip code where "madman" had his computer, as well as his internet service provider. The only problem was that Yahoo!'s corporate offices were in California, where it was 6:30 a.m.

Agents reached a colleague in Sacramento, California, who had a contact at Yahoo!. By 11 a.m. Eastern Time, the Pittsburgh agents had their suspect's IP address. They contacted his internet service provider. The account was registered to thirty-eight-year-old Scott Tyree, of Herndon, Virginia. Holtz contacted the FBI office in Washington, DC. Soon, a team of agents knocked on the door of Tyree's house. When there was no answer, they burst through the front door with guns drawn. Upstairs, they found Alicia, terrified, but alive. She had been chained to the floor, abused and tortured for nearly four days. Now she was safe.[2]

FBI agents found Tyree at his office less than an hour later. The quiet, pony-tailed computer programmer lived a double life. He had no previous criminal convictions, and had a twelve-year-old daughter who lived with his ex-wife. Tyree was arrested, convicted, and imprisoned.

Keep Yourself Safe

- Never give out personal information such as your name, home address, school name, or telephone number in a chat room or on bulletin boards. Never send a picture of yourself to someone you chat with on the computer without a parent or guardian's permission.
- Use screen names that do not reveal your gender.
- Don't keep an online relationship a secret, even if the other person asks you to.
- Do not meet someone or have him or her visit you without the permission of your parent or guardian. If you do choose to meet someone you have met online in person, make sure that you are accompanied by a responsible adult who can protect you if necessary.
- Tell a parent or guardian right away if you read anything on the internet that makes you feel uncomfortable.
- Remember that people online may not be who they say they are. Someone who says that "she" is a "fourteen-year-old girl" could really be an older man.

Alicia Kozakiewicz, pictured here in 2014, founded the Alicia Project to raise awareness of internet predators and advocate for missing persons.

Online Friendships

Alicia is a survivor, but she did not emerge from her ordeal unscathed. She suffered from post-traumatic stress disorder, a severe anxiety disorder that people sometimes develop after serious traumatic events. She lost large chunks of her memory, which is not an uncommon response. In 2007, when Alicia was nineteen years old, she told her story to a congressional committee, urging them to take legislative action against internet sex predators.

Online friendships are easy to make, but people on the internet aren't always who they say they are. Be careful what you reveal to them.

She described herself as a "typical bored, shy, and lonely child" who turned to the internet to fill her time.[3] She struck up an online friendship with a fourteen-year-old girl named Christine. They shared their dreams, their hopes, their most intimate girlhood secrets. When Alicia discovered that "Christine" was really a thirty-one-year-old man named John, she was angry for a time. But she eventually reconnected with her online friend because, as she said, "Christine was still Christine to me."[4]

Career Information

Cybercriminals are using the expanded use of the internet, and the expanded use of devices that use the internet, to conduct everything from the kidnapping of people to the kidnapping of data. Video game consoles, home security systems, and basic email accounts now number among the tools cybercriminals can use to gain access to your personal information. The rising number of malware and ransomware viruses have taken cybercrime to a new level: crippling entire networks and nearly bankrupting companies. Cybercriminals appear to take joy in what they do and in the relative anonymity with which they commit their crimes. Unlike traditional criminals, cybercriminals typically aren't caught red-handed. Rather, elaborate traps intended to catch what could be one solo criminal or a network of hundreds of criminals must be set by experts.

Career opportunities for computer forensic investigators are growing alongside the growing cyber threats. Banks, large corporations, software companies, and military and law enforcement agencies are all looking for computer forensic investigators.

"There is a huge demand, and a lot more schools have created programs," Nasir Memon, a professor at the Polytechnic Institute of New

York University in Brooklyn told the New York Times. "But to be honest, we're still not producing enough students."[1]

Computer forensic investigators must have a strong background in computer science or information technology. Most jobs require a bachelor's degree in one of these fields; an advanced degree (master of science [MS] or doctorate [PhD]) will improve your chances for advancement and a higher salary.

Nick Robertson, a computer forensics expert in Chicago, Illinois, says that being familiar with software as well as hardware is critical for the job. "In order to properly preserve evidence, you need to go out and properly handle large servers, desktops, laptops. You need to remove hard drives, make [copies] of them and properly document everything you do."[2]

Computer forensic investigators also need strong problem-solving and analytical skills. They must be able to write clearly and explain their conclusions, perhaps as expert witnesses in a court of law.

The job is not for the faint of heart. "You may need to go in at night when no one is around and pop a hard drive out of a machine and pretty quickly dig up some information," Robertson said.[3]

Salaries for computer forensics investigators vary widely depending on education, experience, responsibilities, and the employer.

Many universities offer programs tailored to meet the need to combat the often nameless, faceless predators and thieves who lurk online.

SALARY CHART

Employer	Median Salary[4]
Corporation	$54,178
State or local government	$43,721
Federal government	$59,250
Private	$54,178
Contract	$52,761

The above chart shows median salaries for entry-level forensic computer analysts with bachelor's degrees. The salaries rise into the hundreds of thousands of dollars in the federal, corporate, private, and contract sectors, depending on years of experience, education, and certifications.

The following schools have strong computer science programs in information security:

The City University of New York
John Jay College of Criminal Justice
Digital Forensics and Cybersecurity Programs
524 West 59th. Street
New York, NY 10019
Phone: 212-237-8000
www.jjay.cuny.edu/
master-science-digital-forensics-and-cybersecurity

George Mason University
Department of Computer Science
4400 University Drive MSN 4A5
Fairfax, VA 22030 USA
Phone: 703-993-1530
www.cs.gmu.edu/programs/masters/isa/index.html

Georgia Institute of Technology
Institute for Information Security and Privacy
Klaus Advanced Computing Building
266 Ferst Drive
Atlanta, GA 30332-0765
Phone: 404-385-5466
www.gtisc.gatech.edu

Indiana University
School of Informatics and Computing
Informatics Graduate Office

901 East 10th Street, Room 233
Bloomington, IN 47408
Phone: 812-856-3960
xavier.informatics.indiana.edu/gradsites/security/masters

New York University
The Offensive Security, Incident Response and Internet Security Laboratory (OSIRIS Lab)
isis.poly.edu

Purdue University
Department of Computer Science
305 N. University Street
West Lafayette, IN 47907-2107
Phone: 765-494-6010
www.cs.purdue.edu

A list of colleges accredited by the National Security Agency as Centers of Academic Excellence in Cyber Defense is available at www.iad.gov/nietp/reports/current_cae_designated_institutions.cfm.

Some companies and government agencies require applicants to be a Certified Computer Examiner (CCE). Certification is administered by the International Society of Forensic Computer Examiners (ISFCE).

Cybercrime investigators dive into a dark world, one populated by a vast network of criminals—some of them very dangerous and very committed to protecting their criminal trades and networks. Cybercrime investigators are needed to track down kidnappers, like the one who took Alicia Kozakiewicz. They're needed to track down digital fingerprints and data trails that the average person can't identify. They're needed to trace the thieves of copyrighted material and produce the evidence for court. And now, they're needed to find the culprits behind hacks that threaten personal and financial well-being, as well as those breaches that undermine national governance and security.

CHAPTER NOTES

INTRODUCTION: Computer Forensics: A Digital Crime Scene Investigator

1. Ron Nixon and Dan Browning, "Computers Leave a High-tech Trail of Crime Clues," *Star Tribune: Newspaper of the Twin Cities*, March 31, 2005, Metro edition, p. 14A.

CHAPTER 1. Cybercriminals Take the Bank for the Holidays

1. Jeremy Diamond, "Russian Hacking and the 2016 Election: What You Need to Know," *CNN.com*, December 16, 2016, http://www.cnn.com/2016/12/12/politics/russian-hack-donald-trump-2016-election/.
2. Reuters, "How 1 Arrest Silenced Russian Contacts for Western Cyber Crime Fighters," *Fortune*, February 8, 2017, http://fortune.com/2017/02/08/russia-cyber-security-spies/.
3. Mary Papenfuss, "Hackers Shaking Down Pennsylvania Democrats and U.S. Progressive Groups," *Huffington Post*, March 6, 2017, http://www.huffingtonpost.com/entry/russian-hackers-liberal-groups-pennsylvania-democrats_us_58be0aede4b09ab537d6491a.
4. Benjamin Elgin, Dune Lawrence, Carol Matlack, and Michael Riley, "Missed Alarms and 40 Million

Stolen Credit Card Numbers: How Target Blew It," *Bloomberg*, March 17, 2014, https://www.bloomberg.com/news/articles/2014-03-13/target-missed-warnings-in-epic-hack-of-credit-card-data.

5. Alex Veiga, "Some Banks Reissuing Cards Over Home Depot Breach," *Washington Times*, September 24, 2014, http://www.washingtontimes.com/news/2014/sep/24/some-banks-reissuing-cards-over-home-depot-breach/.
6. Mark Hosenball, "Secret Service Probes Link Between Border Arrests, Target Data Breach," *Reuters*, January 21, 2014, http://www.reuters.com/article/us-target-breach-arrests-idUSBREA0K1L220140121.
7. Brian Krebs, "When Undercover Credit Card Buys Go Bad," *KrebsonSecurity.com*, December 7, 2015, https://krebsonsecurity.com/2015/12/when-undercover-credit-card-buys-go-bad/.
8. Elgin, Lawrence, Matlack, and Riley.

CHAPTER 2. The Early Days of Cybercrime

1. Susan W. Brenner, *Cyber Crime: Criminal Threats from Cyberspace* (Santa Barbara, Calif.: Praeger, 2010), p. 10.
2. Douglas Thomas, *Hacker Culture* (Minneapolis, Minn.: University of Minnesota Press, 2002), p. 18.
3. Douglas Martin, "Joybubbles, 58, Peter Pan of Phone Hackers, Dies," *New York Times*, August 20, 2007, http://www.nytimes.com/2007/08/20/us/20engressia.html.

4. "The Electronic Frontier: The Challenge of Unlawful Conduct Involving the Use of the Internet: A Report of the President's Working Group on Unlawful Conduct on the Internet," *Politechbot.com,* February 2000, http://www.politechbot.com/docs/unlawfulconduct.html.
5. Steven Levy, *Hackers: Heroes of the Computer Revolution* (New York: Anchor/Doubleday Press, 1984), p. 91.
6. Computer Industry Almanac, Inc., "Over 150 Million Internet Users Worldwide at Year-end 1998," http://www.c-i-a.com/pr0499.htm.
7. Paul Mungo and Bryan Clough, *Approaching Zero: The Extraordinary World of Hackers, Phreakers, Virus Writers, and Keyboard Criminals* (New York: Random House, 1992), p. 28.
8. Jamie Murphy, Philip Elmer-DeWitt, and Magda Krance, "Computers: The 414 Gang Strikes Again," *Time,* August 19, 1983, http://www.time.com/time/magazine/article/0,9171,949797-1,00.html.
9. Tom Shea, "The FBI Goes After Hackers: Impeded by Outdated Equipment and Techniques and Hampered by Current Laws, the Famous Federal Police Force Wages War Against Computer Crime," *InfoWorld,* March 26, 1984, p. 38.

CHAPTER 3. The Internet of Things

1. Jacob Morgan, "A Simple Explanation of 'the Internet of Things,'" *Forbes,* May 13, 2014,https://www.forbes.com/sites/jacobmorgan

/2014/05/13/simple-explanation-internet-things-that-anyone-can-understand/#55f049211d09.

2. US Department of Justice, "Creator of Melissa Computer Virus Sentenced to 20 Months in Federal Prison," US Department of Justice press release, http://www.justice.gov/criminal/cyber-crime/melissaSent.htm.
3. Byron Acohido and Jon Swartz, "Botnet Scams Are Exploding," *USA Today,* March 17, 2008, Section: Money, p. 1b.
4. Jose Pagliery, "FBI Teams Up with Hackers to Bust Bank Robbing Botnet," *CNN.com,* October 13, 2015, Section: Tech, http://money.cnn.com/2015/10/13/technology/dridex-botnet/.
5. Torsten Ove, "Extradited Hacker Pleads Guilty to Scamming Delmont Company, Sharon Schools," *Pittsburgh Post-Gazette,* February 8, 2017, http://www.post-gazette.com/local/region/2017/02/08/Extradited-hacker-pleads-guilty-to-scamming-Delmont-company-Sharon-schools/stories/201702080187.
6. Brian Krebs, "KrebsOnSecurity Hit with Record DDoS," *Krebsonsecurity.com,* September 21, 2016, https://krebsonsecurity.com/2016/09/krebsonsecurity-hit-with-record-ddos/.
7. Olivia Solon, "Cyber-Extortionists Targeting the Financial Sector Are Demanding Bitcoin Ransoms," *Bloomberg.com,* September 9, 2015, https://www.bloomberg.com/news/articles/2015-09-09/bitcoin-ddos-ransom-demands-raise-dd4bc-profile?mod=djemRiskCompliance.

CHAPTER 4. Cyberwar

1. Tami Abdollah, "More Than 1,100 Cybersecurity Professionals Are Testing Their Ability to Deal with a Cyberattack, Stemming from Recent High-Profile Breaches Against Health Care Companies and Private Retailers," *U.S. News & World Report / Associated Press,* March 9, 2016, https://www.usnews.com/news/business/articles/2016-03-09/us-cyber-pros-test-skills-in-exercise-meant-to-stop-attacks.
2. Rob Thubron, "A Type of Fileless Malware Related to Stuxnet Has Infected Over 100 Banks Around the World," *Techspot,* February 9, 2017, http://www.techspot.com/news/68098-type-fileless-malware-related-stuxnet-has-infected-over.html.
3. Mark Clayton, "Stuxnet Malware Is 'Weapon' Out to Destroy . . . Iran's Bushehr Nuclear Plant?" *CSMonitor.com,* September 21, 2010, http://www.csmonitor.com/USA/2010/0921/Stuxnet-malware-is-weapon-out-to-destroy-Irans-Bushehr-nuclear-plant.
4. Joseph Menn, "Exclusive: U.S. Tried Stuxnet-Style Campaign Against North Korea But Failed," *Reuters,* May 29, 2015, http://www.reuters.com/article/us-usa-northkorea-stuxnet-idUSKBN0OE2DM20150529.
5. Brian Madison Jones, "Nuclear Arms Race." *World History: The Modern Era,* ABC-CLIO, 2017, worldhistory.abc-clio.com/Search/Display/310836.

6. Jose Pagliery, "The Emergence of the 'Cyber Cold War'," *CNN Tech,* January 19, 2017, http://money.cnn.com/2017/01/19/technology/cyber-cold-war/index.html?iid=EL.
7. John Krige and Naomi Oreskes, *Science and Technology in the Global Cold War* (Cambridge, Mass.: MIT Press, 2014).

CHAPTER 5. Spammed

1. "Public Awareness Advisory Regarding '4-1-9' or 'Advance Fee Fraud' Schemes," *Wayback Machine,* http://web.archive.org/web/20020802151417/http://www.secretservice.gov/alert419.shtml
2. "Phishing," *Federal Trade Commission,* September 2011, https://www.consumer.ftc.gov/articles/0003-phishing.
3. Roy Urrico, "New Phishing Scam Using Microsoft Office 365," *Credit Union Times,* December 13, 2016, http://www.cutimes.com/2016/12/13/new-phishing-scam-using-microsoft-office-365.
4. Monica Anderson, "Many Smartphone Owners Don't Take Steps to Secure Their Devices," *Pew Research Center,* March 15, 2017, http://www.pewresearch.org/fact-tank/2017/03/15/many-smartphone-owners-dont-take-steps-to-secure-their-devices/.
5. Ben Johnson, "How Ransomware Works," *Carbon Black,* September 19, 2016, https://www.carbonblack.com/2016/09/19/how-ransomware-works/.

6. Laura Wagner, "LA Hospital Pays Hackers Nearly $17,000 to Restore Computer Network," *NPR*, February 17, 2016, http://www.npr.org/sections/thetwo-way/2016/02/17/467149625/la-hospital-pays-hackers-nearly-17-000-to-restore-computer-network.
7. "Ransomware 101: What, How, and Why," *Trend Micro*, June 14, 2016, https://www.trendmicro.com/vinfo/us/security/news/cybercrime-and-digital-threats/ransomware-101-what-it-is-and-how-it-works.
8. Robert Hackett, "How to Protect Yourself from Ransomware," *Fortune*, March 13, 2017, http://fortune.com/2017/03/13/ransomware-protection-tips/.
9. "What We Investigate," *FBI.gov*, n.d., https://www.fbi.gov/investigate/cyber.

CHAPTER 6. Internet Piracy and the Culture of Free

1. David Goldman, "One Million People Watched Pirated Copies of the 'Game of Thrones' Premiere," *CNN.com*, April 25, 2016, http://money.cnn.com/2016/04/25/media/game-of-thrones-piracy/.
2. David Goldman, "'Game of Thrones': First Four Episodes Leaked Before Premiere," *CNN.com*, April 13, 2015, http://money.cnn.com/2015/04/12/technology/game-of-thrones-leaked-episodes/?iid=EL.

3. Tufayel Ahmed, "HBO Is Making Life a Lot Harder for 'Game of Thrones' Pirates," *Newsweek,* May 10, 2016, http://www.newsweek.com/hbo-making-life-lot-harder-games-thrones-pirates-457957.
4. H. Maria Perry, "The Consequences of a DMCA Violation," *Legal Beagle,* n.d., http://legalbeagle.com/8335872-consequences-dmca-violation.html.
5. Jethro Mullen, "Court Rejects Kim Dotcom's Appeal Against Extradition to U.S.," *CNN.com,* February 20, 2017, http://money.cnn.com/2017/02/20/technology/kim-dotcom-us-extradition/.
6. Clyde Haberman, "Grappling with the 'Culture of Free' in Napster's Aftermath," *New York Times,* December 7, 2014, https://www.nytimes.com/2014/12/08/technology/grappling-with-the-culture-of-free-in-napsters-aftermath.html.
7. "Kim Dotcom to Appeal Against Verdict That New Zealand Raid Was Legal," *Guardian,* February 19, 2014, https://www.theguardian.com/technology/2014/feb/20/kim-dotcom-to-appeal-verdict-that-raid-on-new-zealand-mansion-was-legal.
8. Eleanor Ainge Roy, "Kim Dotcom Extradition to US Can Go Ahead, New Zealand High Court Rule," *Guardian,* February 19, 2017, https://www.theguardian.com/world/2017/feb/20/kim-dotcom-eligible-for-extradition-to-us-new-zealand-high-court-rules.

CHAPTER 7. Online Criminals and Victims: The World of Cyberpolicing

1. Brad Reagan, "Computer Forensics: The New Fingerprinting," *Popular Mechanics,* June 2006, http://www.popular mechanics.com/technology/how-to/computer-security/ 2672751.
2. "Alicia Kozakiewicz Testimony on Sex Predators Online," posted by Representative Debbie Wasserman Schultz, n.d., http://www.youtube.com/watch?v=vGdldKxPock.
3. Ibid.
4. Nicole Weisensee Egan, "Abducted, Enslaved—and Now Talking About It," *People,* Vol. 67, No. 15, April 16, 2007, http://people.com/archive/abducted-enslaved-and-now-talking-about-it-vol-67-no-15/.

Career Information

1. Christopher Drew, "Wanted: 'Cyber Ninjas,'" *New York Times,* January 3, 2010, p. ED18.
2. Gary Anthes, "So You Want to Be a Digital Detective?" *Computerworld,* Vol. 41, No. 1427, April 2, 2007.
3. Ibid.
4. "Forensic Computer Analyst Salary, Average Salaries by Employer Type," *Payscale.com,* http://www.payscale.com.

GLOSSARY

antivirus software Programs that detect malware and notify the user of its presence. This type of software keeps a database of "fingerprints," or characteristics of known viruses, on file.

bit (BInary DigiT) An individual 1 or 0 in a binary numbering system. It is the smallest unit of digital data.

Bitcoin A type of digital currency in which encryption techniques are used to regulate the generation of units of currency and verify the transfer of funds, operating independently of a central bank.

black hat A malicious hacker (more correctly called cracker) who engages in destructive computer exploits that can result in harm to property and/or people; a bad guy, after the Western film tradition in which the villain wears a black hat.

botnet A network of computers programmed in a way that places them under the control of a malicious hacker.

computer forensics The branch of forensic science having to do with legal evidence found on computers and digital storage media; also known as digital forensics.

copyright The exclusive legal right given to a creator to print, publish, perform, film, or record literary, artistic, or musical material, and to authorize others to do the same.

encryption The conversion of information into a cipher or code that can only be converted to its original form through a special key.

firewall A security system consisting of a combination of hardware and software that limits the exposure of a computer or computer network to attack from malicious hackers.

hacker A person who enjoys exploring the details of computer systems and networks and figuring out how to stretch their capabilities. Although the term has commonly come to mean a person who breaks into computers and computer networks without authorization, the hacker community prefers the term "cracker" for this type of person.

identity theft The act of stealing an individual's personal information (for example, name, Social Security number, credit card number, passport information) with the intent of using that information to commit a crime, usually to gain access to that person's money or to gain other benefits.

intellectual property Creative works that can be owned through copyright.

internet piracy Use of the internet to illegally copy or distribute copyrighted works such as movies or songs.

IP address A unique number that identifies a computer and its location on the internet. It is comparable to a street name and house number.

malware Malicious or harmful software, such as viruses, worms, and Trojan horses.

operating system Software, consisting of programs and data, that manages the resources of a computer.

payload Transmitted data that is the intended message in computing or telecommunications. In computer security, the payload is the part of malware which performs a specific function, such as sending spam or deleting or encrypting data.

phishing Trying to get confidential or personal information, such as passwords or bank account numbers, through an email message that tricks the recipient into releasing the information.

phreaking A slang term describing the activity of a subculture of people who study, experiment with, or explore telecommunications systems.

ransomware Malicious software designed to block access to a computer or computer system until money is paid to release it back to its owner.

security patch A piece of software designed to fix problems with or to update a computer program or its supporting data.

server A computer program that carries out some task on behalf of a user. Computers on which these applications are run are also called servers.

spam Unwanted junk email, usually sent to millions of people, often as a means of phishing or spreading malware.

spyware Software that monitors activity on a computer, such as keyboard and mouse activity. Spyware can record personal information entered into the computer via the keyboard.

Trojan horse A malicious computer program used to hack into a computer by misleading users. The term comes from the ancient Greek story of a giant wooden horse Greeks used to stealthily invade the city of Troy.

warrant An authorization from a court that orders police or investigators to carry out a specific act.

white hat A hacker with good intentions who hacks into systems, with permission, in order to find flaws in the computer network; computer security experts; a good guy, after the Western film tradition in which the hero wears a white hat.

worm A program that reproduces itself across computer networks. It is self-contained and does not need to be part of another program to replicate.

Books

Bossler, Adam M., Thomas J. Holt, and Kathryn C. Seigfried-Spellar. *Cybercrime and Digital Forensics: An Introduction.* New York, NY: Routledge, 2015.

Friedman, Allan, and P. W. Singer. *Cybersecurity and Cyberwar: What Everyone Needs to Know.* Oxford, UK: Oxford University Press, 2014.

Goodman, Marc. *Future Crimes: Everything Is Connected, Everyone Is Vulnerable, and What We Can Do About It.* New York, NY: Doubleday, 2015.

Greenhaven Press. *Cybercrime.* New York, NY: Greenhaven Press, 2016.

Kaplan, Fred. *Dark Territory: The Secret History of Cyber War.* New York, NY: Simon & Schuster, 2016.

Sciandra, Mike. *Cybercrime: Using Computers as Weapons.* New York, NY: Lucent Press, 2017.

Zetter, Kim. *Countdown to Zero Day: Stuxnet and the Launch of the World's First Digital Weapon.* New York, NY: Crown Publishers, 2014.

Websites

Crime Scene Investigator Network

www.crime-scene-investigator.net

Read articles on forensic science subjects, including computer forensics; explore links and courses; and browse resources on how to become a crime scene investigator.

FBI, Cyber Crime

www.fbi.gov/investigate/cyber

The FBI is enhancing the cyber division's investigative capacity to sharpen its focus on intrusions into government and private computer networks. Read information on investigations and current threats and priorities.

International Society of Forensic Computer Examiners (ISFCE)

www.isfce.com

This private organization provides computer examiner certification (CCE), ISFCE training for classroom and distance learning, and laboratory proficiency testing. Learn the professional and ethical standards expected from a certified forensic computer examiner.

Interpol, Cybercrime

www.interpol.int/Crime-areas/Cybercrime/Cybercrime

Interpol is the largest international police organization in the world. Learn about Interpol's role in combatting cybercrime and read the latest news articles on cyber threats and what is being done to fight them.

KrebsonSecurity

krebsonsecurity.com

Brian Krebs is a computer science journalist turned in-depth, independent cybercrime investigator, analyst, and reporter. Learn more about cyber threats and keep up with current cyberattack news.

NSA Day of Cyber

nsadayofcyber.com

This free, online program is sponsored by the National Security Administration and enables students to experience what it's like to be six NSA cyber professions. Students will work through real-life cyber scenarios, learn the skills and tools needed to be an NSA cyber professional, and discover the variety of cybersecurity careers out there.

INDEX

A

Advanced Research Projects Agency Network (ARPANET), 28–29, 51
advance fee scams, 53–55
African Prince scam, 53–55, 57
Akamai content delivery network, 41
Apple II, 29

B

Bitcoin, 42, 59
botnets, 36–37, 39–42

C

Capitol One, 18
Central Intelligence Agency (CIA), 11, 15, 31
Chase, 18
Clinton, Hillary, 14, 15
Cold War, 47, 49, 50–52
computer forensic expert, education and skills needed for the job, 80–81
copyright, what it is, 67
credit card theft, 11–13, 15, 17, 18–21, 26, 44
CryptoWall ransomware, 61
"culture of free," 68, 70
Cyber Cold War, 48–49
cybermissile, 43
cybersecurity drills, 44
Cyber Storm V, 44

D

DD4BC hacking group, 42
Democratic National Committee, 14
Department of Homeland Security, 44
Diamreyan, Okpako Mike, 53–55
Digital Millennium Copyright Act (DMCA), 65–66, 68
distributed denial of service (DDOS) attacks, 40–42
Dotcom, Kim, 68, 70
Dridex malware, 40

E

email scams, how to avoid, 60
Engressia, Joe, 23–24

F

Federal Bureau of Investigation (FBI), 24, 31, 37, 62, 70, 71, 72, 74

FireEye security company, 11, 12–13, 49
firewall, 39
floppy disks, 50

G

Game of Thrones, piracy of episodes, 63, 65–66
Ghinkul, Andrey, 37, 40

H

hacking, history of, 23–24, 28–29, 31
Hodirevski, Andrey, 19
Home Depot, 18
hyperlinks/links, and phishing, 39, 58, 60

I

interconnectedness, and security breaches, 33, 35
internet, history of, 28–29
"internet of things," what it is, 32–33
Iran, 43, 46, 47
Israel, and Operation Olympic Games, 46–47

K

Kozakiewicz, Alicia, 71–72, 74, 77–78, 85
Krebs, Brian, 41

M

mainframe computers, 22, 24
malware, how it works, 11–12
Massachusetts Institute of Technology (MIT), 24
Megaupload, 68

N

North Korea, 47
nuclear weapons, using worms to stop production, 43, 45–47, 52

O

online safety, tips for, 75

P

payloads, 57
personal computers, advent of, 29
phishing, 55, 58, 60
phreaking, 23–24, 55
presidential election of 2016, and Russian hackers, 14–15, 17, 48, 49

R

ransomware, 17, 57, 59, 61–62
Rescator, 19
Russian hackers, 14–15, 17, 18, 19, 48, 49

S

Shadowserver Foundation, 40
Snowden, Edward, 15
Stuxnet, 43, 45–47, 52

T

Target, 2013 malware attack, 11–13, 18, 44
torrent sites, 65
Trump, Donald, 14, 17

U

Ukrainian hackers, 15, 18, 19
US Department of Defense, 28

V

viruses, 17, 26, 35, 36, 57, 61, 79

W

War Games, 31
Wikileaks, 14
worms, 26, 43, 46, 47, 57